Beaches, Bars and Blisters

OF THE ISLE OF WIGHT

Beaches, Bars and Blisters

OF THE ISLE OF WIGHT

David Yates

WATERCOLOURS
Mandy Wheeler

ryelands

First published in Great Britain in 2009
Reprinted 2009

British Library Cataloguing-in-Publication Data
A CIP record for this title is available from the British Library

ISBN 978 1 906551 12 4

RYELANDS
Halsgrove House,
Ryelands Industrial Estate,
Bagley Road, Wellington, Somerset TA21 9PZ
Tel: 01823 653777   Fax: 01823 216796
email: sales@halsgrove.com

Part of the Halsgrove group of companies
Information on all Halsgrove titles is available at:
www.halsgrove.com

Printed and bound by Shortrun Press, Exeter

SYNOPSIS

ACKNOWLEDGEMENTS

I should like to thank all those people who helped me to write this book: Martha Bottrell and Ruth Kennedy in Aberdeen, Eve Townsend in Yeovilton, June and Kate Abbott, Tracey Darcey and Lisa White on the Isle of Wight, Mandy Wheeler for painting so many wonderful watercolours, Simone Whitehurst for producing such beautiful maps and graphic illustrations, and Jimmy Wheeler for the loan of his foot.

I also wish to extend my sincerest thanks to Steven Pugsley and the team at Ryelands for believing in this book almost as much as I do!

Finally, I wish to dedicate this book to my mother who, together with my late father, first brought me to the Isle of Wight.

FOREWORD

David Yates was born in Berkshire in 1957. His parents first carried him to the Isle of Wight the following summer, and his love affair with the island began. David served in the Royal Navy from 1976 to 2000, and saw active service in the Falklands War of 1982 and the First Gulf War of 1991. David's first book, *Bomb Alley*, his personal account of the Falklands War aboard HMS *Antrim*, was published by Pen and Sword Books Ltd in 2006, and he finally realised his dream of moving to the island in the same year.

During the events held to mark the twenty-fifth anniversary of the Falklands War in the summer of 2007, David completed a circumnavigational walk of the Isle of Wight, that he had first tackled in 1983 when trying to re-discover himself after his involvement in the 1982 conflict.

This is only a short story, and should take the average reader about three casual days to finish. Which is about the same time it took David to discover some of the beaches, bars and blisters of the Isle of Wight.

Isle of Wight

CHAPTER ONE

STEEPHILL COVE TO DINOSAUR ISLE

The weather forecast predicted twenty-two degrees centigrade and the possibility of showers. Undeterred by the chance of getting soaked occasionally, I waved goodbye to my mum just after eight o'clock in the morning and set off down the narrow 'Love Lane'. Passing Ventnor Cricket Club, with its unusual bowl-shaped ground, I descended a cascade of irregular steps leading down to Steephill Cove. Apart from two local fishermen unloading their morning's

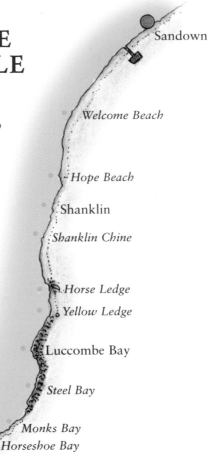

Sandown

Welcome Beach

Hope Beach

Shanklin

Shanklin Chine

Horse Ledge

Yellow Ledge

Luccombe Bay

Steel Bay

Monks Bay

Horseshoe Bay

Wheelers Bay

Ventnor

Steephill Cove

catch of crab and lobsters, the tiny beach was deserted and covered with a light splattering of seaweed from the previous high tide. There was no need to check my map or take any bearings, as for almost all of the circumnavigational walk I was embarking on, I knew that all I had to do was turn left, walk anti-clockwise and keep the sea on my right.

Most of the walk, which would cover approximately seventy miles, would be completed totally unaccompanied, but the prospect of being alone with my thoughts was what I looked forward to. I had tackled many long solo walks in the past, including the entire Lake District, the straits of Gibraltar, and a previous walk round the Isle of Wight in the hot summer of 1983. So the loneliness of long distance walking was not a consideration that filled me with any great trepidation. The 1983 walk had been conducted to help me overcome the effects of my time in the previous year's Falklands War. I felt a similar desire to complete the walk again in 2007, having recently taken part in several high-profile commemorative events, held to mark the twenty-fifth anniversary of the conflict.

I reached the edge of the little cove's rough promenade, and turned round to briefly gaze at the small rocky inlet and handful of assorted cottages nestling below the narrow undercliff like a string of old seashells. My first thoughts of the trip were of how much my ties with the island had changed since the last walk in 1983. Back then, the Isle of Wight had been the annual summer holiday destination for our family at the end of August, and now twenty-four years later, I was setting off from the place where some of the family were now permanently based. Moving away from the idyllic little cove, I covered the short foreshore road to the first climb of the walk, over the lightly rippled concrete track, which snaked steeply up towards the coastal path. I passed a couple of middle-aged people out walking their dogs, and thought how much my youngest daughter's little Lhasa Apso would have loved to have joined me on this walk. However, Molly had short legs, so I knew I would have ended up carrying her under my arm most of the way!

Once on the coastal path, I kept to the twisting tarmac and pebble-dashed path that threaded its way up and down the wooded chalk cliffs, eventually emerging from a tunnel of overhanging bushes where I caught sight of the place where I had spent childhood family holidays of yesteryear – Ventnor. The old

rusting Victorian pier was long gone, but from a distance everything else still looked the same. A steep jumbled terrace of Mediterranean-style properties stretched from the small town above to the narrow strip of finely-pebbled sandy beach at its gently curving base. As I drew nearer, the memories came flooding back. Our young family had poured down to this beautiful haven on the southern tip of the island to spend endless days in the seemingly always-hot sun. Deck-chairing, sand castling and swimming, clambering over the rocks, and eating dripping wet ice creams and fresh bread rolls filled with slices of ham and juicy red tomatoes. I could almost taste the memories as well as visualise the tightly packed groups of people of those times in their brightly striped, highly varnished 'Blake and Spencer' wooden deckchairs on the beach. So different to the rows of white plastic sunbeds that most of their children now lie on each year at some far less attractive beach abroad.

We all loved holidaying at Ventnor, and for two weeks every summer we felt as if we were visiting our second home – which in effect it was – and indeed later on did become. I passed the Spyglass Inn, packed with tourists, on my right, and the Richmond Arms on my left, again pretty busy, but in need of some modernization and a lick of paint. A little further on I stood outside the old Amusement Arcade and heard the sounds of the machines inside as they had always sounded – chirping their chorus of electrical notes to attract the penny-slot gamblers into this mini Las Vegas. Moving just inside the arcade I stood on the exact spot where I must have clutched my old blackened penny as a small curly-haired four-year-old. The memory was so clear I

14

could almost feel the large smooth penny in my hand now, and the fumbling movements it took to bed it into the push-in coin slot of the Laughing Sailor I was attempting to waken from his staring-eyed static pose. I closed my eyes for a few seconds and it felt as if I was actually back there in the scorching hot summer of 1961. As a child, I had pushed the coin in and felt it drop with a hollow 'clunk' somewhere inside, and the sailor started rocking from side to side on his stool as a roar of echoing laughter erupted from his wide, red-lipped wooden mouth. I had taken immediate flight at the shock of what my simple little penny had awakened. I turned sharply and screamed in terror – with my teddy, Shaggy, dangling from one hand, and my other arm outstretched towards my mummy and daddy – whose own laughter matched that of the sailor in the glass-sided navy blue box. I shook my head and laughed a little to myself as I strode away from the arcade, with my small yellow nylon backpack dangling from my hand where Shaggy used to hang.

Passing The Met and The Mill Bay, I left the end of the promenade and passed the spot where the entrance to the old pier used to stand. In its place stood an enormous Victorian-style round-buttressed fort, topped with a bandstand, which had been built to mask the water treatment pump house encased below. We used to love strolling onto the wooden-boarded pier as kids, trying to help our old three-fingered grandad catch the one that always seemed to have just got away. There were few signs of the old pier left now, but just yards further on there was something most certainly still recognisable from my very earliest childhood recollections – the Isle of Wight paddling pool. Thinking back

again to its uniquely shaped island, I wanted to go for a paddle and leap from Ventnor to Shanklin to Godshill like we used to do, and sometimes we would slip and fall in and cry our eyes out. But that would have meant taking my shoes and socks off and losing valuable time, and it was time itself that I was now becoming more aware of as I finished my brief trip back down memory lane in Ventnor.

Due to coastal erosion and the resultant loss of so much crumbling undercliff, the route I now followed took me along the narrow concrete strip of successive coastal protection schemes. The long winding ash-grey promenade and underpinning anti-tank style lumps of triangular-horned moulded rock did not look very attractive, but they were doing their job. I supposed if the rocks had not been laid down like a massive roughcast bandage, this part of the coast might have been washed away years ago, along with all the houses perched like crow's nests on top of it. The long flat promenade was good for walking on, and I quickly lengthened my stride to something closely approaching a loping jog. Back in 1983, I had actually run quite a few sections of the walk, but in the first hour of day one, for the time being I decided against such heroics. The sky was darkening and I could see the tide was almost at its highest mark, which could mean getting wet feet when the path disappeared into the seaweed-covered rocks.

Reaching 'Wheelers Bay' my worst fears were confirmed. Having run out of concrete, I stepped down onto the light shingle beach and then eventually onto no shingle at all – just steep, muddy cliffs and mounds of wet, slippery rocks, over which the waves crashed with repeated showering ferocity. "Damn," I thought, realising that I had made a blunder in not checking the tides. What should I do now? Change my route and head inland up through Bonchurch and along the steeply-wooded coastal path to Shanklin, or just stick with it and try to make it across the rocks all the way around the large hiatus of this major landslip – the much more direct, but potentially wetter route. Looking up to the high slopes of St Boniface Down, I cursed my lack of planning again, yet decided to keep to my basic principle of staying as close to the edge of the island as possible and so started clambering over the rocks towards Shanklin. The rocks were not of even sizes, or easily spaced however, as I found out after crossing only five or six of them, when I lost my footing on a narrow ledge that had looked secure – but wasn't!

I slipped off the rock I was trying to climb, crashed sideways into the foot-deep water and was almost totally covered by the next incoming wave. Yes, I should have ruddy well checked those tides before I set out! Only just avoiding the next incoming wave, I quickly dragged myself to my feet and stood there for a moment, hoping that nobody had seen my fall to earth – or water – then tried to decide what to do next. Oh well, I thought, I'm already wet so I might as well stay in the sea and wade round the rocks instead of trying to clamber over them. That plan sounded fine, and worked well in practice, until I encountered more submerged rocks and fell in again! All thoughts of striding majestically round the island at five miles an hour as I had done back in '83 now disappeared, as I wondered how on earth I was going to complete even the first five miles. Picking myself up again, I wrenched a branch off a large piece of driftwood and used it as a makeshift rock-detector and occasional walking stick. Now with an extra arm, I was able to make some headway and slowly but more surely zigzagged my way carefully in the general direction of the next outcrop of anticipated dry land.

Unfortunately though, as I picked my way steadily past Horseshoe Bay, Monks Bay and then Steel Bay, I found that every supposed 'bay' was in fact nothing much of the sort. Each one proved to be a false outcrop – and what actually lay ahead were many more jagged and slippery rocks, with more rumbling waves crashing over them. After what seemed like ages, I crawled across Luccombe Bay and reached the almost totally submerged Horse Ledge, from where I could now see Shanklin and, further on in the distance, Sandown. Scrambling another couple of hundred yards, I eventually crossed one of the old wooden groynes beneath some spectacular soft red sandstone cliffs and landed on some much sought after shingle, just above the high tide mark. It was 9.50am by my watch. I had probably lost a good half hour from my estimated programme. I checked myself over and found that my three-day-old heavy-duty trainers now looked about twenty years old. My right shin was badly grazed and bleeding from the first fall. I was completely soaked, and so was my backpack, which was also caked in a layer of slimy mud. Fortunately, I had wrapped everything inside the pack in plastic bags before setting off.

Not that I had much inside my bright yellow parachute material backpack. As I laid the contents out to rinse the pack in the sea, I was reminded that I was trying to walk round the island with just a thin cotton wash bag containing a plastic razor, toothbrush and toothpaste, collapsible hairbrush, roll-on deodorant and tiny bottles of shaving oil and shampoo, and that most vital of all items – Johnson's baby oil. A favourite naval tanning oil of mine – if not medically correct! In addition, I had packed some zinc oxide tape, the Ordnance Survey Outdoor Leisure 29 map of the Isle of Wight, notepad and pencil, credit card and cash, a spare pair of socks, shorts and T-shirt, some chewing gum, one half-litre plastic bottle of water, and a thin waterproof jacket. I had not packed a tent, sleeping bag or cooking utensils – or even a small towel. I was also not carrying my mobile phone – or a laptop! On these sorts of walks I prefer to travel as light as possible. Booking into a B&B or hotel at the end of each day is a far less strenuous and much more comfortable way of doing things.

Setting off again at 10.00am with still dripping clothes, I decided to dry myself on the road by picking up my pace along the wide flat promenade that now ran in front of me for about two miles – all the way to the end of Sandown Bay. At this time, on a mid-July morning, Shanklin seafront was just starting to come alive. A trickle of holidaymakers were slowly making their way down to the long sandy beach from their various roosts in the town. As in Ventnor, there were no longer the hordes of young families laden with armfuls of buckets and spades. Most of the young families of Britain now travel to foreign beaches for their warm sand and cool ice creams, where the sun usually shines all day every day. So nearly all the people I saw were the old families, or what was left of them. Old mums and dads, and often just groups of old mums – because their partners had all died long before their times were due – just like my poor old dad had done

himself, at only 63. I thought about my dad quite a bit then for the next mile or so as I remembered all the times he had walked us along this same seafront in his ex-RAF khaki shorts, with his short-sleeved check shirt, grey socks, brightly polished leather sandals and an off-white 'Afrika Corps' forage cap perched on his old bald head. I half expected him to pop out of one of the amusement arcades that I passed and call out,

"Hey David, come and have a go on the Bingo with your old dad. Come on son. Come and win yourself an alarm clock to get you up in the morning."

I certainly felt his spirit with me as I passed by the odd island visitor or two, walking to and fro along the prom. They were mostly older folks with sharply creased trousers or shorts. Some were walking alone, some held hands, and others trailed dogs or licked 99 ice creams. These were the type of people who had not deserted the Isle of Wight since the boom-times had ended, and had helped to preserve a viable tourist economy in most parts of the island. Dad would have enjoyed walking this stretch of the coast with me today I thought, and we would both have had ice cream running down our chins by now I imagined, as I licked my dry lips and stopped to buy – a large 99 cone.

Striding out again, I passed one of the more recent additions to Shanklin beach – a 'Surf Shack'. Here, a couple of heavily-tattooed young guys in their early twenties cavorted among the sleek, multi-coloured boards displaying their tanned and muscular torsos for the girls to see. Without any discernable border, Shanklin promenade then gave way to Sandown's own version, with its similar array of arcades, cafés and bucket-and-spade shops. I passed a pub that reminded me of some of my times in the Royal Navy, The Jolly Sailor. I toyed with the idea of nipping in for a pint, but quickly decided against it in case the walk turned into a one long pub-crawl.

July is normally one of the hottest months of the year, but today, after a week of inclement weather, it was still not particularly warm. A slow procession of fluffy grey clouds cast intermittent shadows on the land, and I thought again of the contrast between our weather, and weather on the continent and further abroad. To my left I came across Brown's old golf course, a weed-choked boating lake, and further ahead a rather tired-looking Sandown Zoo, with its flapping union jack and weathered concrete tiger perched on top of the crumbling battlement-style façade of its converted fort entrance. We had visited these old attractions as children, but they looked far less appealing today. But all is not lost. People are trying hard to resurrect the phoenix from the ashes. Between the boating lake and the zoo, a gigantic stylised model of a Pterodactyl rose above the entrance to Dinosaur Isle. Often referred to as the fossil capital of Europe, the entrepreneurial market of the Isle of Wight is now in full swing in its attempts to attract younger holidaymakers. It is possible that these visitors will even find their own fossils on the beaches. What child would want to lie, bored, on a foreign sun-lounger, when they could discover massive dinosaurs on their own holiday doorstep!

Isle of Wight

CHAPTER TWO

DINOSAUR ISLE TO RYDE

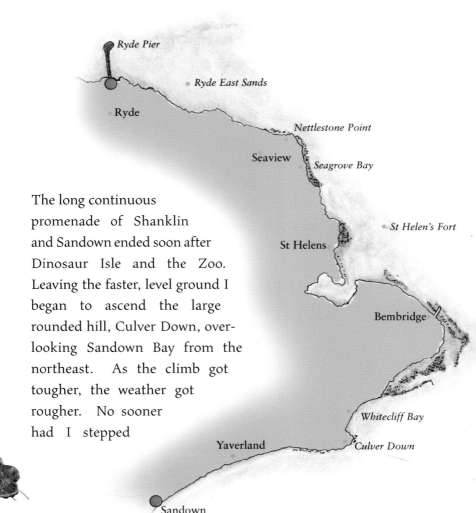

The long continuous promenade of Shanklin and Sandown ended soon after Dinosaur Isle and the Zoo. Leaving the faster, level ground I began to ascend the large rounded hill, Culver Down, over-looking Sandown Bay from the northeast. As the climb got tougher, the weather got rougher. No sooner had I stepped from tarmac onto grass than the clouds darkened and started shedding their contents all over me. I pulled out my light rain-proof jacket, though there was little point because I was still soaked through from my scramble in the sea. However, it did help to keep me a bit warmer, for as the rain fell so did the temperature. I was not the only person to be caught out on an exposed walk, as I soon met a family coming down the hill with no coats on at all. The mother followed behind at the back smiling sweetly at me, giving me one of those shrugs that said, 'I told him we should have brought our jackets.'

Culver Down was not too steep however. With the rain keeping me cool, I soon wound my way up the well-beaten track to the top where I found a large monument, erected in 1845, for someone called Charles Pelham, the Earl of Yarborough – in the lee of which two other walkers were sheltering.

"You walking round the island?" one of them called out as I moved closer to read the inscription.

"Yeah that's right," I replied, "I'm trying to go round in three days like I did a few years ago."

These two much more heavily-laden men sounded quite impressed by this bold statement of intent – especially when they saw the sparse amount of gear I had flung over one shoulder.

"Ah, but you're not roughing it like us are you lad," one of them taunted.

"No way," I responded, moving off down the track again, "That's far too much like hard work for my liking, I want a soft bed and a shower each night, not just a sleeping bag and a bird bath in a sink thanks very much."

These were the first 'serious' hikers I had encountered on the walk, and judging by my previous attempt in '83, I knew they would not be the last. However, I did wonder which was the most popular way round the island, anti-clockwise as I had done then and was doing now, or clockwise, as they were doing. I didn't suppose it mattered really, because the principle I had started out with was just the same whichever direction you chose, – for you always kept the sea to the same side. I was glad I was not carrying a tent and kitchen gear though. No wonder they both looked rather dirty and tired.

As if to reinforce this belief, and with the gentle slope now working in my favour, I soon decided to use the momentum it was

providing to break into a light jog. After jogging all the way to the bottom of the Down I was pleasantly surprised to find that I had not actually lost too much fitness since 1983. I was now 49 and not just 25 and approaching my prime as I had been then, but I was not bearing up too badly – especially thinking back to the two men at the monument, who both looked a lot younger than me, but a lot less fit too. That was what the good healthy living in the Navy had done for me. All that rugby, fitness training, partying and chasing girls in every port! A perfect way of keeping fit, I thought, as my legs began to tighten a little when I reached the flat ground approaching the holiday camp at Whitecliff Bay. I started walking again in case anyone saw me and thought I was an escaped prisoner from the Isle of Wight's Parkhurst Prison or somewhere equally secure.

The holiday camp looked exactly like what it really was – a throwback to the heydays in the fifties and sixties, with numerous small white caravans strung about the site. I saw a few people milling around outside their 'vans', but because of the continuing drizzle I imagined that most inhabitants were inside watching the cricket on TV. Seeing a little bit of civilization again after being away from it for the course of Culver Down also made me think of my rumbling stomach, especially as the position of the sun told me it was approaching lunchtime. I was not carrying any food, so I just made do by draining the contents of my bottle of water, wiping my lips dry and forcing myself on, in the sure knowledge that there was bound to be somewhere to buy something to eat as I skirted round the edge of Bembridge town itself. Although I knew from the map that the town was not very far away, I also knew that distances on the map can often be deceptive. I found this out to my hungry cost on this particular stretch of path, which wound in and out like a giant tape worm between a wet tunnel of overhanging bushes and stinging nettles.

On this section of my walk I also began to notice the major geographical difference between 1983 and now, namely the vast amount of coastal erosion that had taken place in the intervening years. Edging around Bembridge Public School playing fields, there were several graphic examples of nature's environmental revenge. It looked as if an enormous sea monster had crept up in the night and taken great chunks out of the coastline of chalky rocks and windswept bushy trees. The path ran in a northerly direction for a while, then disappeared crumbling into the sea before fresh forest posts and barbed wire forced me back in almost the reverse direction until I picked up the original path again, and came upon a fresh landslip and another detour. The first and most obvious questions I asked myself at these stages were, "How long has this been going on?" and, "What's to stop the sea monster eventually eating up the entire island?"

The crumbling path ended and the outskirts of Bembridge came into view as I followed the signposts directing me through a sedate old housing estate until I reached the coastline again and saw a completely different view from the one I had left a mile away. Instead of a clear expanse of English Channel over my right shoulder, I could now see in the distance the West Sussex coastline almost as far as Brighton. Much closer, in a northerly direction towards Portsmouth, arose the closest of the Solent forts – one of Lord Palmerston's 1870 follies, St Helen's Fort, the scene of the annual fort walk, where some three-thousand people file out to the fort on a narrow sandbank during the lowest tide of the year.

With the change of view also came a change of housing, as the previous chain of holiday camp caravans and small private houses were now replaced by much larger properties along the Bembridge foreshore. No doubt these were all former residences of the old Victorian admirals who had retired to the island to reside in modest little mansions by the sea where they could still survey the Home Fleet as it made its way in and out of Portsmouth Harbour. Many of them no doubt hoisted union jacks in their front gardens and saluted each passing Dreadnought as it belched out its great clouds of black smoke on its way to perform yet another piece of gunboat diplomacy in defence of the Empire.

The beach in front of these giant houses even had its own set of matching grand wooden beach huts set out in a row on the edge of the sands. But of course, none of them appeared to be in use because there was no fleet at sea today to toast with raised glasses of champagne. Taking a short cut across the shoreline at this point, I found another reason why this previously popular resort was now almost deserted, for the beach looked like one giant rotting brown pancake – and smelled like it too. I often like to amble along foreshores beachcombing for items washed up on the last tide, but the only things I encountered on this short passage were what looked like the remnants of an old car ferry, with lights, tyres and even a rusting steering wheel stuck firmly in the muddy sand at one point. It's little wonder that places like this are no longer packed with summer visitors, when they can now enjoy

much less flotsam and jetsam on a much hotter beach in the Mediterranean.

I arrived at the stage of the walk where I knew from previous experience that a potential short cut could be taken by wading across a river inlet instead of following the road and bridge around it. However, seeing the muddy state of the riverbank, it did not take too long to decide which option to take. It was just as well that I took the longer road and bridge route, or I would have missed the little waterside snack bar. I didn't pause to eat much in the snack bar, for I had already calculated that three Mars bars and a bottle of water should see me all right until I reached my intended destination for lunch, opposite Ryde pier. So, three bars of chocolate I ate whilst walking on, washed down by a litre of cold bottled water, from a Highland spring near where I had once lived in Scotland.

I wasn't carrying a mobile phone, so a short distance further on I was fortunate enough to find a red telephone box that I could use to check in with mum back at Steephill Cove.

"Hi mum," I yelled, "It's me. I've just stopped for a bite to eat at Bembridge Point."

" Oh, it's only twenty to one. My, you have done well," she replied, "Any blisters yet?"

I said I had none yet, but thinking about it I realised that I actually had, because of the soaking I had picked up earlier. Since then, the 'so-called' heavyweight training shoes had squelched their way back to relative dryness at the expense of my poor wrinkled and abused toes. "No, I'm fine mum. I'll be in Ryde soon and then stop for lunch."

I think mum was pretty impressed by the progress I was making, and come to think of it I was fairly pleased too. I had not set any strict daily targets for my walk, but when I looked at the opened map, I felt that to walk from Steephill Cove to Ryde pier in one morning was not too bad going.

Skirting around the edge of Bembridge Harbour I was struck by the strange array of eccentric old houseboats moored end-on to the ragged perimeter of the inlet. There were vessels, which looked as if they had played some part in the evacuation of Dunkirk or the D-Day landings, and others advertising B&B or Tea Rooms. There were also interspersed hulks and skeletons of former floating palaces – all now rotting slowly away and covered in a bright overcoat of green and brown seaweed. I deviated from the coastal path for a mile or so as I cut inland to walk through St Helens, before picking the path up again at St Helen's church.

There I followed the route past another holiday centre, through Priory Woods and around Seagrove Bay to reach Seaview and the old promenade at Nettlestone Point. Here I saw several wealthy-looking people strolling along the prom adjacent to the 'members only' Seaview Yacht Club. There were signs of money around here all right. On the foreshore there was a sign saying that local residents maintained the shingle, and looking at the size of some of the local houses, it was easy to see how the occupants could afford to pay to have a daily refuse collection from their own front door steps.

It was now half past one and my legs were feeling a little weary as I stepped down onto the wide expanse of Ryde East Sands and caught my first glance of the long tentacle of Ryde pier stretching

out into the Solent over three miles away. Glancing across to Portsmouth, I could see the large spinnaker tower at Gunwharf Quays. The millennium tower had not been built in July 1982 when I returned from the Falklands War. I stopped and stared at the stretch of water and the final course that HMS *Antrim* had steered that day to bring most of us safely home from the conflict 8,000 miles away in the South Atlantic. As always on these occasions, the hairs on the back of my neck rose as I remembered the air-sea battle in Bomb Alley and all the other good and bad times down south. It had been an incredible homecoming; a flotilla of small craft escorted us in and the massive crowds cheered for all their worth on the shores of Southsea and Gosport. I wiped a small tear from my eye. Attending many of the recent commemorative events to mark the twenty-fifth anniversary of the Falklands War had brought back so many memories, and now I was hopeful that this second walk around the island would, like it's predecessor in 1983, help to heal some of the re-opened emotional wounds.

I started walking once more. On the opposite coastline at the southern tip of the New Forest, I could see the giant cigarette-shaped chimney of Fawley Power Station. I had walked these sands as a boy many times in the past, and played for ages in the shallow waters that eventually drained away to such an extent that I used to think I would be able to walk all the way across to Portsmouth. Of course not, but sometimes, when the tide was really low you could trot out about two miles into the Solent, and on certain days of the year games of cricket could even be played on the sandbank right in the middle! But now the skies were darkening again and I wanted to reach the pier before the rains came down and soaked me for a third time. With only two hundred yards to go it had just started spitting as I took a chance and jogged across the hovercraft pad. I carried on jogging until I passed under the 1824 pier and checked the time on my watch as one of the old London underground trains passed overhead. Twenty past two it said. And remarkably, despite the drenchings, I had managed to cover eighteen miles in just over six hours. I congratulated myself on this minor achievement and made my way off the beach to seek refuge in the King Lud, crossing the road as the heavens finally opened in earnest. Inside the bar, a few other people must have been equally glad to see the rain, for a small queue had formed to wait for the lone barmaid's methodical but smiling service. I felt a bit touristy and scruffy in my walking gear, but none of the others were dressed up either, so I unloaded my backpack and reached for my small wallet and one of the ten pound notes inside.

I took my first sip of cider, then a longer cool gulp and felt it tingle my tonsils as it passed down my dry throat and into my empty stomach. Certainly, I had had three Mars bars and drunk a couple of bottles of water, but I was still in need of a proper drink after a hard morning's walk. "Oh, and food," I thought. "What shall I have?" Trying to keep to the light lunchtime diet I had promised myself, I decided not to order one of the bar lunches chalked on the blackboard. Instead I just ordered a single packet of peanuts to replace some of the lost energy and salt that the eighteen miles had extracted from my body, with the promise of an apple or two for pudding later on in town.

Nibbling my peanuts and sipping my cider, I idly looked around the bar at the other lunchtime drinkers. An assortment of pensioners, manual workers and office staff, with a couple of odd-looking holidaymakers like myself eyeing up the fixtures and fittings and pictures, and the other people in the bar. I noticed two young girls on the stools next to mine – shabbily dressed in jeans and 'biker' T-shirts, looking like they were in here for the afternoon.

I considered staying for the same amount of time as I polished off the cider, but opted to try and find some fruit and retire to the beach for an hour or so instead. However, once I reached the door I could see it was not going to be a beachy sort of day, and quickly made a dash up the high street to another pub, the Royal Squadron.

This place was traditionally 'themed' in terms of design and

35

decoration, with loud Radio One music booming from speakers all around the bar. Looking at the tariff blackboards, I could also see that this place was much cheaper than the last, for an extended happy hour was being promoted — with some beers on offer at only £1.25 per pint instead of normally double that price. I ordered a pint of beer this time, and a second packet of peanuts, then sat on another, taller stool to sip my second pint of the day and munch my way through another packet of nutrients and salt. Because of the lower prices, the Royal Squadron was much busier than the King Lud, although the mixture of drinkers was roughly the same, and included an Irish contingent across the bar from me — two couples who had clearly been there for much longer than just two pints and a few packets of peanuts.

Sailors, or rather ex-sailors, and Irishmen are like magnets in a bar. You cannot keep them apart. Even if they don't know the other person's origins when they walk in to the bar, it never seems to take too long for either party to find out. Sailors and Irishmen, you see, have an awful lot in common in terms of enjoying the worldly delights of the inside of a bar. Both like drinking and eyeing up the girls, telling jokes and performing silly little party tricks, and making feeble efforts to Indian arm wrestle or balance a stool on the end of their nose. Because of this magnetism, I just could not help but introduce myself when one of them came over to the bar and ordered two pints of the 'black stuff' and a couple of Bloody Marys. Or Bloody Fairies as he referred to them under his breath as he shook his head and reached for some change from the large pocket of coins that dragged his trousers down at one side.

"Hi" I said, sticking out my hand, "How d'ya do. My name's

Rowdy Yates. Are you on holiday here?"

'Bryan' introduced himself, and then, as is always the way with these magnetic meetings we quickly established that I was an ex-matelot and therefore entitled to offer my hand to an unknown Irishman in a strange bar. Then we did the next thing that always occurs when such meetings take place, we stood and told jokes – Irish jokes. Over the next hour or so I was allowed to tell all the Irish jokes I knew. Bryan and his wife and friends told all the ones they knew too, as I joined in their round of drinks and ordered a couple of Bloody Fairies the next time it was my turn to withdraw another ten pound note.

Eventually the Irish quartet said they had to leave and meet some more friends for a drink up the road. Feeling the walk round the island could suddenly grind to a halt in Ryde if I accepted their invitation to join them, I grudgingly declined their offer and left at the same time as they did, to complete my lunchtime dietary requirements by buying a couple of apples and a bag of monkey nuts to chew on the beach, which now basked in sunshine and promised to remain so for the next few hours. I must have had about six or seven pints that lunchtime, and to say it relaxed me would be an understatement, because, with the sea far away in the distance, I had only just settled into a nice sunny position on top of a large wooden groyne when I promptly fell asleep – as a result of the long walk from Steephill Cove to Ryde, of course!

CHAPTER THREE

RYDE TO EAST COWES

I must have slept for over two hours on that large wooden sand-stopping structure one hundred yards from Ryde pier, for when I eventually woke, the tide was beginning to lap the furthest reach of the groyne, less than ten feet away. I looked at my watch – ten to five already. Time I got up and got walking again. But with a head that was still spinning a bit, and parts of me that had been burned under the hot rays, I thought, "Oh just a couple of minutes longer. A couple of extra minutes lying on my red sunburned tummy won't hurt." Turning over, I was both careful to make sure I did not topple off the six-foot high groyne, and could hardly believe that I had managed to tightrope my way along it in the first place in my partially inebriated state. It's amazing what tricks an ex-Royal Navy 'matelot' can get up to when he is 'sailing a little close to the wind'. I was reminded of the Irish quartet in the Royal Squadron and started to chuckle to myself at the laughs we had – largely at their own nation's expense.

Gazing out across the incoming sea covering Ryde West Sands, I noticed the odd scattering of people going about whatever business it was they were going about, on the edge of the advancing tide. Two young girls threatened to stop the incoming waves altogether by digging a long moat. A couple walked hand in hand with their jeans rolled up to their knees. More unusually, I saw a turbaned woman in her mid-fifties strolling along in a light-coloured sarong with a plastic carrier bag flapping in the light breeze, and bending down occasionally to collect something from the damp sands below her sandal-clad feet. I say turbaned and sarong-adorned, and you might imagine that I had seen an Asian woman, but not so, for approaching the height of an English summer (cloudy skies and all) I saw a distinguished-looking white woman with a turban on her head! I was longing to run across and ask the turbaned woman what it was she was collecting in her little bag – especially if it was some sort of seafood that I might be invited home to sample. No, I sighed, she would not be my type, not with something like that on her head. Even if she was approachable, she probably still would not want to invite a beer-smelling, ex-matelot back to her designer-furnished seaside terrace for a gin and tonic and whatever fresh fruits of the sea it was she had collected.

I lay on the groyne for another twenty minutes watching the trains trundle back and forth along the pier and a party of Spanish schoolgirls performing like a circus troupe on the dry sandy beach beneath the old metal Victorian structure. I could tell they were Spanish, not only by the occasional dialect that I picked up, but also by their looks, and the appearance of their teachers and chaperones, who guarded their young Catholic charges with the intensity normally preserved for high category prisoners in an exercise yard. I would definitely not be going over to practice my extremely limited Spanish on that bunch of fourteen or fifteen year old schoolgirls, I thought, not without risking being attacked by eight eagle-eyed matriarchs.

With a swiftly sobering mind, I strolled along the narrow path that took me out of Ryde, north of Binstead and past Quarr Abbey at a quarter to six, where a band of merry monks lived – no doubt praying for more rain on that hot, sunny afternoon. The coastal path led me to Fishbourne and the entrance to the car ferry terminal. It was here that I had arrived from, and set off for Portsmouth on so many occasions in the past. Passing the queue of traffic approaching the ferry, my mind went back to one particularly memorable occasion in August 1970, when we were returning to the mainland after our summer holidays and dad had an 'altercation' with a man who was unhappy at the length of time he was waiting to board a ferry. Dad had not done anything to offend the man. He had just picked on our car to highlight his protest against the car park attendants.

The situation got quite heated, and the man stood for ages shouting and waving his arms and blocking our path when the attendants were frustratingly waving us on. Getting fed-up himself, dad edged our car forward to such an extent that the chap leapt up and sat on our bonnet. When that happened the rest of us in the car thought dad would explode, but surprisingly he did not. He just seized the opportunity to shoot down to the bottom of the long sloping car park – with the man clutching onto the windscreen wipers for dear life! The irate man exploded then, and we all screamed as we thought this lunatic would now attack our dad, but fortunately the attendants wrestled him away from our car to speak to a policeman who had just arrived on the scene. As I reached the short bridge crossing Wootton Creek I could see the funny side of my dad's actions that day, and I also remember getting ready to dive out of the car and rugby tackle the man to the ground – though I was only twelve at the time!

As I strode up the hill towards a fish and chip shop, the approaching smell banished all thoughts of 1970, as my brain switched into 'feed me' mode instead. It was now over ten hours since breakfast. I had walked about twenty miles and all I had eaten were three Mars bars, a couple of packets of peanuts, two apples and a bag of roasted monkey nuts. As a result, I was ready to eat a whole whale and chips, never mind just ordinary cod or haddock. As a result of being so ravenous, I ordered two large portions of fish and chips when I reached the front of the queue. No sooner had I left the shop with my paper bundle under my arm than I ripped it open and started devouring the steaming contents – just like a man who had not eaten proper food for ten hours! Between great mouthfuls of hot food I cooled myself down with two tins of fizzy lemonade, as I sat on a wall adjacent to the chip shop, watching the rush hour traffic pass before me to and from Ryde. I say rush hour, although being such a small island there are never any real log-jams like there are on the mainland. There are no motorways and only one small stretch of dual carriageway. Getting stuck behind a herd of cows down a narrow country lane might be an occasional hazard, but delays caused by too much traffic on the roads seldom are.

My meal finally over, and my sore, sunburned tummy full, I set off back down the hill to connect up with the coastal path once more. Having stopped for twenty minutes, and now totally sobered up, I noticed how stiff my legs and hips had become. Gone was the spring lamb feeling of the early hours, and in its place was a sensation that felt as if a circle of donkeys had repeatedly kicked me all the way from my waist down. With the time reaching half past six, I started looking out for a B&B to finish my walking for the day and rest my weary limbs. But no such signs were in evidence as I left the main road and picked up the path again as it weaved its way through the quiet back streets of Wootton, past Palmer's Farm and along the Brocks Copse road. Looking at the map as the houses finally ran out, I realised I would be extremely lucky to find any accommodation along this seemingly long and winding narrow lane. So, despite my sore joints, I picked up my pace as best as I could and strode out for the place where I knew I would find a bed somewhere – East Cowes.

I did not see anyone along that road, which seemed to go on and on forever. A couple of cars passed by though, and at one stage I almost thought of trying to hitch a lift because my legs were becoming so heavy, but I gritted my teeth, smiled politely and continued putting one tired foot in front of another until I eventually reached the main road again just outside Whippingham. Crossing the road, I walked on another mile and a half until I came to the entrance of the old residence where Queen Victoria had lived from 1845, until her death in 1901 – Osborne House. Back in 1983, I had not taken this easy front door route to the house. Trying to keep as close as I could to the water's edge, I had left the coastal path at Wootton to follow the creek back to the Solent. From there I had followed the ragged rock-covered foreshore and eventually arrived at the backdoor of Osborne House, where I had to try and explain how I had got in without paying! Crossing King's Quay just before the grounds of Queen Victoria's island retreat had resulted in me getting plastered in thick mud up to the bottom of my skimpy swimming trunks – which smelled terrible by the time I reached the astonished lady in the ticket office on my way out.

Just past Osborne House I reached the outskirts of East Cowes, and some twenty sore and limping minutes later I finally arrived at the small floating bridge that would have taken me across the River Medina. Would that is, had I arrived about one minute earlier, for I had just missed the latest sailing across the narrow strip of water that separates East and West Cowes. Checking the timetable, I was not prepared to wait another fifteen minutes for the ferry to come back again, so I decided to bring my day's walk to a halt on the east side of the river. Turning away from the ferry I slowly scoured the quiet local streets looking for any B&B signs until I finally found one not far from The White Hart, where I rang the doorbell and stood waiting for an answer, feeling as though I could not walk another inch. Eventually a tall man came to the door and showed me one of the rooms he had vacant. The room did not look too inspiring and the shower was downstairs next to the kitchen, but there was a choice of a double or single bed and both looked like they would make excellent companions that night. I paid him his thirty pounds, closed the door and collapsed in a heap on one of the beds. I must have lain there for ten minutes or so, until I felt that I must get cleaned up before going to bed. I quickly unpacked and tiptoed barefoot down the stairs to scrub off some of the grime of the day.

The hot water brought some life back to my exhausted limbs and I felt much better once I had got cleaned up and dried off. Then it was time to deal with my laundry. As I said before, I had brought only one spare set of clothes, so getting my first set washed and dried overnight was a key part of my lightweight walking strategy. I filled the sink with hot water and rubbed the tiny tablet of courtesy soap to produce a bit of lather, then pushed my clothes into the basin and left them to soak for a few minutes while I switched on the TV to watch the nine o'clock news. Unfortunately however, watching the news on that set was almost impossible because the screen flickered and jumped with poor reception, especially whenever a lorry rolled up into the East Cowes ferry car park, which was directly outside my open bedroom window. In the absence of a decent TV or any good book to read, I decided to go for a nightcap in the town – or what I thought would be the town. Washing my clothes out, I then hung them over the cold radiator to dry (suspecting that they might not do so successfully) and limped back down the stairs to seek the bright lights of East Cowes. At this point my whole body from my middle downwards felt even more stiff and sore than before, and I now hobbled along like someone who had twice been attacked by a circle of donkeys in the same day.

I eventually dropped in for a pint at each of the three pubs that I could find open, but they were all very quiet and I kept yawning and wincing every time I moved. It did not take too long to decide that enough was enough and that I was ready to climb into one of the beds at the B&B and watch a little more flickering TV, while more lorries used their loud air brakes outside my window. Once I had actually trailed back along the road and up the stairs, I waived the idea of playing with the TV aerial. After walking 26 miles from Steephill Cove to East Cowes, I just wanted to lie down and sleep. My last thoughts were of a couple more Irish jokes that I had forgotten to tell at lunchtime.

CHAPTER FOUR

EAST COWES TO YARMOUTH

I elected to sleep in the single bed that night, and although it was closer to the open window above the lorry park, it did draw in the cool night air and was as soft as sleeping on a pile of eider feathers. I slept like a log until half past six, and woke up feeling as stiff as a log too! So stiff in fact that I began to have serious doubts as to whether I would be able to walk back to the chain ferry – let alone another twenty miles, as I had originally envisaged. Gingerly I rolled out of bed and stood up to do some stretching exercises to try to put some life back in to my creaking body. I had used this little routine for years and it

had often come in handy on previous occasions. Starting from the top I began with neck-twists, bends and nods, then stretching and swinging my arms back and forwards. After that I worked on my 'abdoms' for a while – again performing a combination of twists, bends and stretches.

With the top half of my body now awake and feeling much looser, I concentrated on my hips and legs, which felt like a solid lump of concrete compared to the rest of my rejuvenated body. I started by doing some rocking movements to ease the stiffness from my hips, then some wide-legged pelvic thrusts (which would have looked very strange to anyone watching from outside). Then I spent a good ten minutes stretching and massaging the parts of my body which had taken the vast majority of punishment the day before – my poor old legs. I kept punishing my lower limbs until they were tingling all over with hot, searing pains. Not feeling any muscle or tendon pulls, I knew without the pain there would be no gain. True to previous tried and tested form, the pain did achieve some gain, for at the end of my twenty minute session in front of the mirror my legs felt as though they might just have another day or two left in them after all.

With my body back in some order, I checked the set of clothes I had washed in the sink last night and hung optimistically on the radiator to dry. As expected they were still damp. But looking out of the window, the weather did not look too bad so I guessed they would soon dry off if I strung them from my backpack later on as I walked in the open country beyond West Cowes.

I had shaved yesterday evening, so all I did to clean myself up this morning was brush my teeth and plunge my head in a basin of warm water to freshen myself up a bit. After that I applied a liberal smearing of roll-on deodorant, threw on the spare set of clothes, stuffed the rest of my gear in the backpack (including the damp clothes inside a polythene bag), and tiptoed down the stairs for breakfast. A giant, sullen-looking youth who looked a bit like 'Lurch' out of the 'Addams Family' greeted me at the entrance to the dining room, pointed to my small table and said,

"What can I get you? A full cooked breakfast and toast?"

I replied that I would just have the toast and help myself to the cereals.

To which he muttered, "Fine," and lurched off to the kitchen, no doubt glad that he had been spared the delicate task of breaking an egg – which for his size of hands must have been a daunting prospect at this especially drowsy time of the morning.

Like the rest of the house, the dining room was not very inspiring. Whilst my table itself was clean and neatly laid, the rest of the room resembled a country farmer's office, with cardboard boxes and piles of old magazines and a multitude of other clutter lying all over the place. I thought briefly how it certainly would not have passed one of my Warrant Officer's catering inspections in the Navy. But then I was not there to shine my torch around and scribble notes on a clipboard. I was there to start the day with as much cereal and toast as I could possibly eat. Sipping three small glasses of 'fresh' packet orange juice, four soggy Weetabix were quickly scraped from my bowl, then four slices of jam-covered toast. A whole pot of coffee washed it all down and I was ready for the road once more. "Cheers that was lovely," I called out as I stood to leave the room.

Leaving the B&B behind me, I eased myself back into walking mode by taking a slow hike to the chain ferry, where after waiting for a few minutes I caught the eight o'clock across to West Cowes. The ferry was fairly busy at that time of a morning, with lots of people in smart suits or other working clothes making their way dolefully towards another day's toil somewhere. There were also a couple of cyclists on the ferry, and I looked enviously at the gleaming bikes which would have provided so much relief today, rather than treading the solid roads and paths as I was about to do at the start of my second day.

On the other side of the Medina River we all streamed off the ferry and I carried on walking straight through the middle of the town. As if I did not know it already, I was reminded just how different West Cowes and East Cowes are in terms of the type of properties and the overall 'ambience' of the surrounding architecture. East Cowes looked drab and uninspiring, especially at the end of a long hard slog. West Cowes was like a breath of fresh air and I regretted not having waited for that next ferry last night after all. On this side of the river I was sure I could have found a much better B&B. On the other hand, if I had made it across I might have gone out for more drinks than I had last night, and then I might not have got up so early or enthusiastically as I had done this morning. So I put the timing of the ferry down to fate, increased the length and pace of my stride and forged my way along the pedestrianised high street until it brought me to Cowes Castle and the home of the Royal Yacht Squadron. This is where I saw how much West and East Cowes *really* differed. Instead of a noisy lorry park, this side of the river had the exclusive

RYS Club House, frequented by dandily dressed 'yachties', unlike the other side, with its groups of cigarette-puffing lorry drivers and queue of cars heading for Southampton.

I passed a large pub on my left hand side, outside which sat two or three little huddles of coffee-drinkers wearing sunglasses, looking like they were trying to bring some sense to their heads after a heavy night on the tiles the previous evening. I did not feel at all hungover myself, and having stopped briefly to buy a small bottle of water, I knew that I should be all right for liquid refreshment for a few miles. I had studied the map quite closely before going to bed the previous night and I was not at all sure then how far I would be able to make it on the aching legs that were seizing up like oil-excluded pistons. I still hoped to keep to some sort of mental target by walking another seventeen miles to Yarmouth if it was at all possible. Strolling along the promenade looking at the early morning yachts in the Solent on my right, and the row of large yachting mansions on my left, I made a quick assessment of how far I might actually be able to walk before my legs seized up once more. My hips felt loose enough, the thighs too and even my dodgy left knee was not aching as much as it did before. So I thought, I would just give it all I've got and see how far I could go. I certainly did not expect to walk too much further than Yarmouth, or reach anywhere near the twenty-six miles of yesterday, but a decent fifteen miles or so would not be too bad.

Egypt Point, at the tip of the promenade, the most northerly point of the island, gave me a good long flat start to my second day's walking. When I saw a couple of joggers I was even tempted for one moment to join them for a mile or so to see what reserves

I might have in the old pins. I decided against that in case I burnt myself out too early. Instead, at the end of the large row of big houses, I took the damp clothes out and tied them loosely to the backpack so that they would dry in the stiffening breeze. There were far fewer people at this end of the prom, just a few dog-walkers were out with their well-groomed toy poodles and highland terriers. There were no mongrels to be seen on this west side of the river. One or two walkers looked in my direction as I passed them, but the majority kept about their business, well their dogs' business anyway, which they slung from their spare hands in little polythene bags. Some even carried little coloured pooper-scoopers, although I never actually saw anyone bold enough to use one on the clean shingle in my scruffy presence. If one or two had bigger scoopers, I'm sure they would have lifted me up into a bag too. What, a common hiker with clothes flapping from his backpack to dry – on our Royal promenade! Whatever next. We should form a committee about this!

Reaching Gurnard Bay, I followed the path slightly inland to pass through the small village of Gurnard Marsh. A somewhat eccentric-looking place, with one particular old wooden seafront hut sporting a collection of TV star gnomes outside. There was even one group, which resembled the characters of Dad's Army. Good heavens above, I thought, what would Captain Mainwaring have said if he had known that his intrepid platoon of Home Guard heroes had been turned into garden gnomes!

"Don't be ridiculous Pike! Get these gnomes out of this garden now do you hear. Come on Godfrey and Frazer, stop dithering around like a couple of old women, give him a hand, but be careful with that one who looks a bit like me. He seems to be quite distinguished don't you think?"

At ten past nine I left the foreshore of Gurnard Bay and came across something equally bizarre as the chorus line of celebrity gnomes – a row of very old and largely forgotten holiday villas. I say forgotten, because being mostly covered in a matted covering of brambles, the collection of old wooden structures and railway carriages just beyond Cliff Farm did have a certain air of the *Marie Celeste* about them. As if some had been locked up at the end of one final long hot summer, and never re-opened by their winter-felled owners in the spring. One string of old huts gave the impression that a Victorian steam engine had puffed its last iron lungs of grey cloudy vapour across the field, before unshackling its load behind it and shooting over the cliffs to a watery oblivion. The scene looked very sad, as I imagined all the cheerful holidays that must have been enjoyed in these tiny wooden sanctuaries by the sea – long before the days of package tours and foreign timeshares in far grander quarters than old railway carriages.

The coastal path snaked its way in a south-westerly direction around the edge of Thorness Bay, where I spotted a couple of wind-surfers out to play in the stiff breezes that funneled into this flat and exposed section of island coastline. They were not dressed in Bermuda shorts and Ray Bans for, although this was the height of the English summer, out of necessity they sported coloured wet suits instead. Leaving the last camper van with a roof rack and board on top behind me, I followed the path inland again – right through the middle of the Haven holiday camp. Here I felt a little out of place with my shirt and socks still flapping limply from my bright yellow backpack, and I received a few staring glances from the visitors who were far more appropriately attired for this communal type of holiday-making in their cream coloured shorts and bright motif T shirts. I nodded a few times and danced round a couple of children on their bikes, then I was through the camp and over a stile and back on to a more familiar earth path again.

I say earth, for that is what it was under my feet as I followed the old narrow winding field tracks across and around the edges of a succession of fields. In these thickly hedged places, neglected by any consistent or sufficient rainfall for some time, the earth I now trod on was beginning to look like the surface of another planet. The dry conditions had drawn nearly all the wet spring's moisture out of the soil, then cracked and split it into an enormous grid of crazy-paved and pockmarked slabs. Not only had the earth divided into millions of different pieces, it had also buckled and twisted, leaving a path that presented a trip hazard at every other stride. I twisted my ankles a few times over the next few minutes, and it was with no regrets that I finally left the low-level assault course behind me, clambered over a last remaining stile at Little Whitehouse and was able to walk safely on flat tarmac again.

At this point, I should point out once more that this was not the exact route I had followed back in 1983. For then, seeking to walk round the *entire* island, I had not cut in at the holiday camp as I had today. Instead I had carried on round the coast across a terrible stretch of rocky shoreline until I came to a massive fence that proclaimed 'MOD PROPERTY – KEEP OUT'. I had seen the indications for such a restricted area on the map, but somehow, thinking that it would not actually be that difficult, I had hoped to reach the sandy section of beach that lay further ahead, then possibly wade across the Newtown river and thereby keep to the island's edge. The idea of chopping a few miles off the official coastal path backfired when it took me ages to cross the mile of rocks, then more time to brush my way through the badly overgrown woods back to where I now stood as I reached the tiny hamlet of Porchfield.

I assessed Porchfield to be a hamlet, because I only saw about thirty houses from the road – but strangely enough two different public telephones. It made me laugh a bit seeing those, when I thought back to the times when I scampered down the gangway of a ship of 480 men to queue at one of only four telephone boxes provided for the entire ship's company! A traditional red phone box was set outside a pub I recognised from my previous walk and several car journeys before and since – The Sportsman's Rest. I thought of going inside, but again my common sense persuaded me not to and I swept past the oasis, sipping water from my bottle and thinking of lunchtime when I would not need to toss a coin to make that decision.

Passing by an old cemetery displaying a sign, 'No Dogs' and a rather large lady arranging border flowers in her front garden surrounded by a small feline guard of cats, I approached a War Memorial to those local inhabitants lost in the Great and Second World Wars. Every time I come across one of these familiar monuments I stop for a moment and read the names etched into the face of the stone. Particularly in tiny places like Porchfield, I am always astounded by the degree of loss suffered by such small and isolated communities. I have been in two much smaller wars myself, and it never ceases to amaze me how many lives have been lost in each of the World Wars. I had visited the battlefields of northern France with my dad and brother on a bicycling youth hostel tour in 1978, and was deeply shocked by the level of slaughter recorded on the stomach-churning number of stones and crosses that mark the graves of those who could be pulled from the appalling Flanders mud. But this was no Loos cemetery, or any of the many others we saw around the fields where my old Scottish granddad had crashed to the ground with a German bullet through his right shoulder. This was a tiny hamlet on the

Isle of Wight, where a mere handful of simple country dwellings had lost the lives of eleven of their finest young men in two bloody wars.

The road then took me past an equally familiar, though much more refreshing landmark that I recognised. I came across two leafy woods, described on the map as Windgate and then Walter's Copse. I knew of copses from my days at home in the Berkshire countryside, and I also knew how a properly maintained wood of hazel had once been invaluable to all rural communities. For once harvested, this somewhat unusual crop could be turned by skilled hands into all manner of different types of fencing and baskets and pegs and other implements for domestic or industrial use. What I most remembered about hazel from my youth was that it made excellent walking sticks – with lovely comfortable handles.

Jumping over a dry, shallow ditch, I selected a likely-looking branch rising up from the base of a clump of young hazel, bent it forward so far with my hands until I could jump on it at the bottom and prise it away from its parent at the roots. This left me with a green-leafed branch of about fifteen feet long. I broke off the unwanted part of the branch and the leafy residue to leave myself with a stick about four feet long. All I had to do then was drag it along the hard ground to grind off the roots from the handle and scrape off the bark, and my walking stick would be complete. The only snag was that I did not have a knife with me to strip off the bark, so instead I resorted to the method I had occasionally used in the past – stripping it off with my thumb nails! This was a long slow task, that took nearly three miles to finish off, but once complete and well ground down on the road,

I was then able to hold aloft a walking stick that an old woodsman would have been proud to sell to any passing pilgrim.

Apart from stripping my hazel stick, this section of road was one of the least interesting parts of the coastal path, and hard on my legs too, which had felt much better once I had left Cowes. However, the map indicated that I would soon be able to take a short cut across some fields, so when the entrance finally appeared, my soles heaved a sigh of relief as the three-mile stretch of tarmac came to an end and a much softer meadow took its place. The little path across the fields led me directly to a small place called Newtown, which had once been the capital of the island. I arrived at precisely four minutes to one. Unfortunately, once I reached Newtown I was then back on the hard road again for more toe-grinding miles. Up until then my toes had not felt too bad in comparison with the rest of my legs, but on the roads I could feel that some more zinc oxide tape would be required the next time I stopped for a rest.

Passing one o'clock, my stomach was beginning to rumble quite a bit too as I had not found anywhere to buy something to eat all morning. I could have had a snack at the Sportsman's Rest, but I was afraid that the smell of beer might have been too overpowering to resist. Now I regretted that decision, and draining the last of my litre of water, I knew it would not be too long before my dry lips would tell me I needed some liquid refreshment.

Maybe the lack of food and water started to play tricks on my mind then, for feeling confident with just the very occasional glance at the map, I managed to get lost for the first time since starting off on the previous day. Somehow, I thought I had passed through the small village of Shalfleet without noticing it, then took the right-hand path to what I assumed would be Lower Hamstead. I was a clear mile or so further on, before I finally realised that I was not heading for Lower Hamstead. I was on my way to the remote Shalfleet Quay, which had no connecting path back onto the correct route!

As it turned out, once I realised my mistake I was not too downhearted because this little unplanned detour actually contained some of the nicest scenery on the island, – a point testified by the number of artists working away on the banks of the estuary, which fed from the Newtown river. I stopped to examine a few of the paintings being created on canvas. Most were depictions of small boats and landscapes, and to my untrained eye they all seemed to be the works of a new Constable or Turner. Although I stopped to repair my blistered toes and clarify directions, I did not pause any longer to enjoy the idyllic little spot. In fact I did not pause anywhere at all for long, because instead of walking back to the spot where I had taken the wrong direction, with new life back in my toes, I broke into my first light jog of today's walk.

It was quite hot in the midday sun, and I had not run anywhere properly for ages, so it came as quite a surprise when not only did I feel comfortable running, but I also felt amazingly light on my feet. In fact jogging almost felt easier than foot slogging, especially along the hard uneven track. I had been walking a mile every fifteen to sixteen minutes at that stage, but mainly because I wanted to make up for lost time, I jogged the mile back to the road in only eight minutes. What was not so impressive was my degree of thirst at the end of it.

Picking the path up again from where I had left it when I got lost, I quickly re-established my bearings and headed off in the right direction to Shalfleet, where I found the next coastal path sign, complete with a '6 miles to Yarmouth' marker on it. That information made me wince a little bit as I still had not found any food or water, and I estimated that I had at least another hour and a quarter to walk. Just as I climbed over the stile that took me off the road and into a big sloping field, a van-load of long-haired hippies in wash-dyed shirts passed by, tooting their horn and waving like maniacs. They were no doubt on a tour of the island themselves, trying to encourage those on foot to seek some karma with mother earth. I waved back, and wished the hippies had stopped to give me a lift to the Sportsman's Rest or somewhere equally wet and inviting. But they did not stop of course, so I stripped off my T-shirt under the hot sun, and resigned myself to walking this last stretch – without anything to eat or drink.

The path now took me down the side of the large sloping field, where I again used gravity to help me jog to the bottom. I crossed a tiny tributary of the Newtown river by means of a footbridge made of old railway sleepers. Quite a large number of these old sleepers showed signs of having been used to support a railway line, and maybe that explained why the row of carriages I had seen earlier had run out of track!

Across the bridge, I followed a winding path for a short distance through some woods until it joined a wider, straight gravel path that, after one initial long curved bend, took me up a straight and relatively steep piece of track for over two miles. Boxed in by tall trees on either side for most of this section, the walk was again a little tedious, and with the slope working against me, it was also quite hard work on tired legs and an empty stomach.

This was probably the cause of what followed. When arriving at what I thought was Hamstead Farm, for some reason, after patting a couple of small wiry dogs on the way, I took the right fork instead of the left and ended up walking another mile in the wrong direction. I could have kicked myself when I realised what I had done, and felt such a fool because the sea had been on my left side instead of my right, so there was really no excuse for getting it wrong. Turning around, I jogged for a short while until the path became too steep, then dragged my feet the last few yards back to the eager company of the two farm dogs. "Thanks for letting me know I was going down the wrong path chaps," I jokingly called out as they both licked my hand in anticipation of receiving some titbits – which I would have eaten myself if I had had any.

I retraced my steps a little further, and came upon the signpost I was looking for: 'Yarmouth 2¼ miles'. The correct path took me over a long narrow meadow with a couple of horses in it, and then over another dried-out trip-hazard of a field, before I came across a mansion that appeared to have been recently built in an isolated country position. It looked just like the sort of dream-home you would ask for if you won the lottery. That thought got me thinking about my own brush with the golden hand of fate a few summers ago when I came close to winning the lottery myself.

I was staying at mum's house at Steephill Cove at the time, lying upstairs watching TV, when the numbers started tumbling. I had a ticket with six lines on it for the office syndicate that I ran, so when the balls started dropping I quickly ran my eyes up and down the ticket looking for any matching numbers. Out came the first ball, and I ringed a number. Out came the second, and I ringed two further numbers. Then out came the third ball, and I ringed a third number on one of the lines and called across to my son, "Hey we've won a tenner." Then the fourth ball came out, also on the same line, and I shouted, "Bloody hell, that's four now." Then the fifth ball rolled along and it was also on the same line and my heart started thumping like crazy. I shouted even louder, "BLOODY HELL, NOW WE'VE GOT FIVE AND JUST NEED NUMBER FORTY TWO FOR THE JACKPOT." All the forty-series balls are blue, so when the sixth ball dropped out and I saw that it was blue, I almost fainted. Then I felt as sick as a parrot as 'the voice of the balls' called out, "Forty." I could have cried, but then I realised that we still had a chance of the bonus ball. Would you believe it, another blue ball dropped down, and as it rolled along the shute I was sure it was forty-two. When it stopped rolling my heart sank for the second and last time when I saw it was forty-five. We had been so close. So close to winning enough money to have a mansion built like the one I had just passed – with the double garage and maybe six bathrooms, and no doubt an indoor swimming pool too. So close. I shook my head again in disbelief that we had won only £1,200, when a couple of numbers either way could have materialised so many of our family's wildest dreams.

My feet were feeling really tired when I passed the mansion, and my spirits were down a bit because of the thought of how close I had come to owning a place like that myself. Then I saw another signpost that made my spirits sink even lower. I could not believe my eyes when the next marker read, '2 ½ miles to Yarmouth'! "Oh, you must be joking ref," I shouted in frustration. I just could not understand how I had walked another mile and yet a quarter of a mile had been *added* to the distance left to walk for my lunch! Checking the map, I realised that perhaps the first signpost had been somewhat optimistic. Feeling that luck was well and truly against me, I nonetheless bit the bullet one more time and pushed on along the twisting track of Bouldnor Forest, where the air hung with the fresh smell of pine trees and bark chippings. The path looked fairly new in some sections of the forest, and after a short distance it was quite easy to see why.

As in other places I had seen already, the great sea monster of coastal erosion was also eating into this part of the coastline. When the route of the path took me to the edge of the forest, I could even see the monster at work in the waters below me. Small, almost un-noticed lapping waves, rich with the colour of orange and brown sand and clay, nibbled slowly away at the roots of the next line of pine trees.

Just when I thought this leg of the journey would never end, I reached the end of the forest, walked a quarter of a mile up the road and entered the town that I had been dreaming of for the past four hours: Yarmouth. Although I felt completely 'all-in', I discovered a slight skip in my last few steps. I took great pride in the fact that I *had* given it a good go after leaving Cowes feeling

like a casualty. Instead of flaking out at the end of the prom as I first expected, I had actually managed to walk the incredible distance of seventeen miles to Yarmouth – albeit with a couple of mistaken detours along the way!

Isle of Wight

East Cowes
Ryde
Yarmouth
Freshwater
Sandown
Chale
Steephill Cove

CHAPTER FIVE

YARMOUTH TO FRESHWATER

Feeling like a man who *had* just walked about ten miles without any food and drink, my first priority on arriving at Yarmouth was to sort that out. I topped up my plastic bottle with chalky-tasting water from a tap that I had recently passed by. However, I still raced into

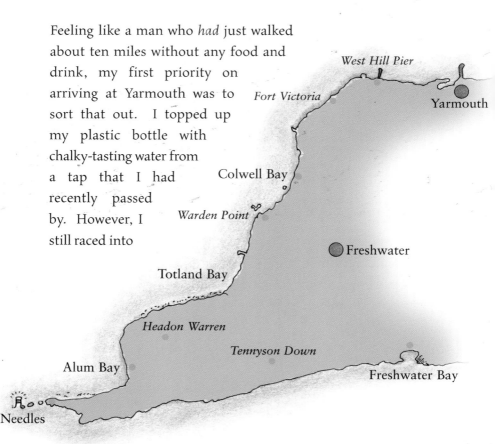

West Hill Pier

Fort Victoria

Yarmouth

Colwell Bay

Warden Point

Freshwater

Totland Bay

Headon Warren

Tennyson Down

Alum Bay

Freshwater Bay

Needles

the first little newsagent's shop I came across to get some proper bottled water, plus two Snickers bars and three small ripe bananas. The first bar of chocolate disappeared outside the shop even before I started walking again, followed by a banana, the other bar of chocolate and then the other two bananas, all in the space of about two minutes! I checked my watch: two o'clock – time for a quick pint. Walking a short distance along the road I went into the Kings Head, stood my stick and backpack in a corner and ordered a pint of cider. Sitting down, I breezed through *The Times* newspaper, that I had picked up with the food, catching up on world news and sipping my ice cold drink in between pages.

Next I pulled the map out again and studied how far I thought I could walk during the rest of the afternoon. My feet, or rather a few of my toes, felt a bit sore, but although the rest of my legs felt 'tight', I still appeared to have no serious injuries. Deciding to have only one pint of cider, I calculated that I might just be able to walk the ten miles or so to the next place that would have accommodation – Freshwater Bay. Draining the last drops and leaving the paper behind for someone else, I stepped out onto the road again, weaved in and out of the tourists strolling along window shopping, and set off on the fourth leg of my journey. However, I noticed that whilst my throat and stomach had been refreshed, my poor old toes were now biting back with a vengeance.

I hobbled this way and that, hoping they would bed themselves in again, but by the time I got to West Hill pier about a mile away, it was quite clear that some more urgent and lasting 'running' repairs were required.

Un-lacing my trainers, I suspected the worst when I saw the mottled red and blue stains at the end of each low-ankle sock. The blue I recognised as dye from my useless footwear, but I groaned when I realised that the red was blood from my damaged toes. Peeling both socks off, my fears were confirmed as I gazed down at ten toes that were starting to look like ripe red chillies, blistered so much that the skin had all come off on the inside of my socks! I shuffled down the last two yards of shingle to the water, and plunged both feet in the sea to ponder what to do next. The cold water refreshed and no doubt cleaned the toes, but I knew I would have to do some pretty good first aid to patch them up enough to walk much further.

I drew my feet out of the water and dried them on my shirt, and carefully set about wrapping up my toes like an Egyptian might embalm a dead Pharaoh!

I tackled one toe at a time, strapping it up as best as I could with zinc oxide tape, then securing it to one of its neighbours. Already feeling much better, I cushioned my feet even further by putting on *both* pairs of socks. Lacing up the trainers as tight as I could, my feet felt almost like new. Whilst I knew I would suffer for a few days at the end of the walk, I felt confident that I should be able to make it to Freshwater Bay at least. I learned a very obvious lesson at that moment that I should have known already. Always tackle long walks in footwear that has been thoroughly tried and tested before, and not just used for a couple of training walks before the start. My 'so-called' heavy-duty trainers now had great splits in both soles, and I could not just go and change them at the shop!

From my impromptu field hospital on West Hill beach, the path took me up past the old ramparts of Fort Victoria, then through Fort Victoria country park, from where I enjoyed a really close view of Hurst Castle, less than one mile away on the other side of the narrowing Solent. Seeing the castle so near to the island made me wonder why nobody had tried to build a bridge across this short stretch of water. I had heard various stories of people designing all sorts of bold schemes to cross the Solent at other places, but although the mainland had far less well-developed road and rail connections at this point, it looked like the ideal spot from my primitive engineer's eye-view.

I was making fairly good speed on my 'new' feet, and raced past Brambles holiday camp and down onto the southeasterly end of Colwell Bay – which looked as lovely as I could always remember it from my childhood. Ventnor was our favourite place, but if we were dragged away for a day trip, Colwell Bay was often the most called-for second choice. The picturesque sandy bay had hardly changed since the 1960s, and appeared to be as popular with young families now as it was then. Weaving my way through the mass of promenade deckchairs and beach towels, and taking the path round the next piece of headland at Warden Point, I could see one of the island's most famous natural landmarks: the Needles – sticking up from the sea like a row of massive white stalagmites. Away in the distance on the mainland I was also sure I could just see Bournemouth and Swanage. Walking along very close to the water's edge, I arrived at Totland Bay where I knew I would be enjoying my last bit of flat ground – probably until I reached Freshwater. I looked closely at everything I could see in this latest little sandy bay, a once-proud Victorian pier, a row of wooden groynes, small groups of sunbathers and children skimming stones on the water. Passing the Waterfront Bar, the flat concrete came to an abrupt end and my first steep path of the afternoon beckoned. Shuffling my backpack and slapping my thighs as I started my first ascent, I drew deep breaths and knew that the hardest physical challenge of the walk was about to begin.

The fairly exacting scramble took me quickly away from the shoreline flora I had become so used to over most of my walk, to cut through surroundings that were more familiar in my former adopted Scottish homeland, as I passed through some of the prettiest purple heather I have ever seen in any highland glen, or even in a garden centre. I picked a tiny sprig and tucked it in my backpack for luck, then made my way across more heather and gorse bushes as I climbed Headon Warren. The top of the Warren sported an Iron Age barrow, where the sign said that 'faggots' of sticks had been kept in readiness for lighting to warn of attack by invaders from the sea. Standing by the barrow it was easy to see why this particular position had been chosen. I could not only pick out Swanage quite clearly to the west, but I could also scan back across the entire length of the island to the east – and out to sea almost to the coast of France. The panoramic view was tremendous, and probably the best such view on the island. But I could not afford to stay too long because it was also a very exposed spot, and despite the frequent sunny intervals it was still pretty chilly in the racing wind that shot across the top of the hill.

Having climbed over 360 feet to Headon Warren, I now had to climb down the other side. This should have been less strenuous,

but was actually much trickier. For whilst I was swiftly going downhill, the path had so many twists and turns in it I ended up feeling like a skier in a downhill event. Once again, because of the dry weather, the path was badly cracked. At one point I nearly broke my ankle and crashed into a mass of stinging nettles. Fortunately my 'third leg', the sturdy hazel walking stick, saved me.

Passing the edge of a small golf course, I made my final descent and approach to what is probably the most commercialised tourist resort on the island: Alum Bay. This is the place where the different coloured sands come from to make those little glass ornaments you see on so many mantelpieces around the country. I did not have time to go into the visitor attraction, and having only been there the previous summer with my youngest daughter, I felt no need to refresh my memory. We had done all the touristy type of things at Alum Bay, including the mini Las Vegas of amusement arcades, walking down the steep Alum Bay Chine, admiring the view of the Needles from the pebble beach at the bottom, then catching the chairlift back up to the top. After that we had gone into the souvenir shops and rounded off our visit by making a couple of those little glass ornaments, expertly spooning in any colour combinations we liked, before a young girl rammed a bit more sand in and sealed the bottom tightly. With those thoughts in my mind, I crossed the coach park and took the path up to the high grassland downs. Moving easily up the track, then path, I came under the barrage

of the stiffening breeze that I had first detected up at the Warren. It was now blowing straight at me, making me bend into it slightly as I made my way up above Alum Bay to the coastguard cottages on the tip of West High down.

At twenty past five I reached a point on the down where another impressive panoramic scene opened up before me, for now, looking in a distant easterly direction, I could see St Catherine's lighthouse at the bottom corner of the island. I knew that St Catherine's was less than five miles from where I had set off at Steephill Cove. The sight and thought of almost being able to see the finishing line filled me with an amazing sense of exhilaration and achievement. Although I knew I still had many long miles to go, I also knew the end of my walk would never be far from view from now on. I was so happy at breaking the crest of the down and seeing the finishing line almost in sight that I celebrated by tucking my thumbs in my backpack straps and jogged the next downhill section for half a mile. I felt brilliant! The air was rushing past my body, and I forgot all about my raw toes as my legs carried me swiftly across Tennyson Down to the monument at the top. I cannot profess to know any of Tennyson's work – apart that is from a few often mis-quoted lines from his famous *Charge of the Light Brigade*. I suspected he must have been quite an inspirational character in the fast-developing Victorian world he lived in. I read on the monument that the Poet Laureate died in 1892, the same year my Scottish grandad was born. That left me thinking he also provided a link to my own past. Although they could never have met, I wondered if my grandad had ever considered any of Tennyson's great words when he had crouched below the parapet at Loos very early that damp September morning in 1915, when Rudyard Kipling's son and the Queen Mother's brother fell amongst the other heavy casualties who were mown down like autumn wheat that day.

I had not thought of Tennyson's words before the time of my own battles in the Falklands and Gulf wars, but thinking of them now, I realised the prophetic lines would have struck an inspiring but fearful chord had someone read them aloud to us over the ship's broadcast. Other thoughts raced through my head as I rode into my own valleys of death at South Georgia, the Falkland Islands and off the coast of Iraqi-held Saudi Arabia. As I walked slowly away from the monument, I wondered what words my son would consider if he were ever called upon to charge into his own valley of death like the 600 brave souls of Queen Victoria's Light Brigade.

Having checked my map to see that it showed the monument was one of the highest points on the island at 482 feet, I knew that the rest of my walk today could only be downhill. I walked a little further and saw Freshwater Bay clearly below me, and I also knew it should be downhill all the way to my next fish and chip feast somewhere in the next hour or so. I had bought enough water in Yarmouth to see me to the end of the day, but not wanting to stop and nibble every few miles, I had deliberately refrained from bringing any more food. The prospect of another massive couple of fish and chip suppers and a nice comfy bed increasingly filled my thoughts from then on.

Making my way down the easterly side of the Down, although still buffeted by the wind, I lightly jogged from time to time as underfoot conditions allowed. I quickly made my way down the last two miles to the bottom of the down and into Freshwater Bay for ten past six, where I was reminded of other childhood memories. Freshwater is a very apt description for the little bay, for my overriding memory of this place is that the seawater was very refreshing indeed! We used to come here occasionally as a family, and we had a good time throwing pebbles in the sea and bravely swimming in the water that was always cold – no matter how hot it was on the shingle beach.

Freshwater Bay was also the place where I first saw another human being outside of my own family in the nude. Back in the summer of 1970, around 500,000 flower-loving hippies flocked to Afton Down near Freshwater for one of the last original Isle of Wight pop festivals, featuring Jimi Hendrix, The Who and The Doors. As was the wont of hippies in those days, after a few odd-smelling cigarettes, one particular group of 'long haired yobbos' (as my dad called them) suddenly peeled all their clothes off not far from where we were licking our ice creams. This immediately prompted mum and dad to usher us off the beach as quickly as their widely draped towels would herd us – doing their best to cover our eyes!

Feeling my walking for the day was surely over, I decided to sit a while on the familiar old beach. Knowing how refreshing the sea was, I also whipped my shoes and socks off again to give my sore digits one last cold bath of seawater before going off to find some filling fish and chips and a cosy place to stay. I sat with my feet in the water for almost fifteen minutes, and threw endless pebbles in the ice-cold sea. Then, when my toes started to go numb with the cold I re-dressed my wounds (which thankfully were no worse) and headed off the beach to find the next two things on my mental shopping list. A group of teenage skateboarders were running and slapping their boards up and down the short promenade, so I stopped one to ask for directions.

"Excuse me mate – any idea where I can get some fish and chips round here?"

The lad started to reply on his own, but was quickly supported by the other skateboarders, who all seemed keen to do their good deed for the day.

"Just up the road there mate, past that telephone box, and then see where that car's turning? Well just down there about half a mile and you'll find the chippy opposite a pub."

"Yeah, that's right," the others echoed, "Just up the road past the phone box and turn down that road where the car's going."

I stopped at the phone box to ring mum, then took the route that the kids had given me. After what seemed a lot longer than half a mile, I stopped to ask a taxi driver where the chip shop was. Looking a bit hacked off that I was not asking for a lift anywhere, the driver huffed,

"Along this road a bit further, then take the second on the right, and it's just along the road on your left – just opposite a pub."

I set off again, with increasing hunger, and I picked up the pace a bit more, certain that I could taste the first chips in less than five minutes. Once more I walked much further than I thought the taxi driver had indicated, so yet again I stopped to ask directions, this time from a young papergirl.

"Excuse me love, could you point me in the direction of your local chippy please." Seeing that I had nodded in the direction that I was walking in, the girl replied,

"Well, it's not up there. You need to go back down the road, and after about half a mile you should see a sign into the village. Take that road, and the chippy is just past the garage."

I explained how it looked like I had been given one or two run-a-rounds by the previous fish and chip shop guides, but the girl was only about fourteen, with smudged mascara and blue-painted nails, so she just giggled in a fourteen-year old girl way, and skipped up the next garden path on her round. Despite believing that the young girl had given me the correct directions, I swear I must still have walked at least another mile before I came to rely on other senses that told me a fish and chip shop was nearby – I could now smell it! Less than two hundred yards later there it was, past a garage and opposite a pub – just like they all said it would be!

There was no queue when I finally dragged my tired legs into the chip shop, so scanning the overhead menu board I ordered double fish and chips, mushy peas and curry sauce – and two cans of fizzy orange. Then with the massive paper bundle in one hand and my backpack and stick in the other, I hobbled across the road to a long wooden seat. The chips were lovely. Big and fat, and well cooked – just as I like them. The fish was good too; huge slabs of haddock, in a golden crispy batter with lots of vinegar. The mushy peas in batter and curry sauce were fine, and in a short time I had eaten the whole lot and washed it down with the two cans of fizzy orange.

Fed and watered, now I looked around for signs of any B&B boards, and saw a potential one just fifty yards down the road in the shape of the 'Royal Standard Hotel'. When I came to rise from the seat, I found I had a bit of a problem. I could hardly stand up, let alone move, because my legs had almost totally seized up! During the time it had taken me to eat my giant meal, it felt as if someone had come along and secretly encased my lower limbs in a large concrete cast. They were stiff and really sore too; every muscle and sinew seemed to be screaming out, 'no more, no more, we just can't take any more!' Somehow, I managed to shuffle along to the Standard, and once inside with a pint of cider sitting in front of me, I booked into a single room for the sum of only £30. I would have paid a lot more than that; because there was just no way I was going to go 'shopping around' for anything else in my condition. No, £30 for the night would be just fine, I thought, as I drained the cider and stepped very slowly up the stairs to my room. For the price, the room was not too bad at all, and it was certainly a whole sight better than the one I had stayed in the night before. It had a TV that did not flicker, that I tested fully within five minutes, as soon as I had unpacked and crashed out onto the bed to watch Eastenders at eight o'clock. I had walked twenty eight miles on my second day of the trip, and despite getting lost or misdirected three times, and with some very raw toes, I was confident that I would still be able to complete my walk around the island on day three.

Isle of Wight

East Cowes
Ryde
Yarmouth
Freshwater
Sandown
Chale
Steephill Cove

CHAPTER SIX

FRESHWATER TO CHALE

I fell asleep last night watching the TV in my room, and only vaguely remember waking up at some unearthly hour to switch it off again before returning stiffly to the land of soft un-walking dreams. My watch alarm woke me at 7.30am, and I dragged myself out of bed, and went through my limbering up exercises as I had done the previous morning in East Cowes. This time, the joints took far longer to loosen up and there were numerous new blisters to cover with fresh layers of zinc oxide tape. I finally made it down for breakfast at 8.50am, and sat in a

Freshwater

Freshwater Bay

Shippards Chine
Hanover Point
Fossil Forest

Chilton Chine   Grange Farm

Cowleaze Chine
Shepherd's Chine

Whale Chine   Chale

large comfortable dining room for fifteen minutes consuming as much orange juice, muesli, wholemeal toast and jam as my stomach would allow. My only companions in the room were a businessman in a suit munching away on fried bread whilst speaking to someone on his mobile phone, and a large black gentleman who looked like a doctor, judging by the size and quality of the shiny black briefcase at his side. I even wondered if he would mind looking at my toes, but reckoned that he probably would not appreciate examining my over-ripened tomatoes – not when he had just consumed two of his own with his large cooked breakfast!

I left the Royal Standard Hotel at precisely 9.10am. My feet had collected a few more areas of pain overnight, but at least this would definitely be the last day of the walk, even if I had to crawl the final few miles back to Steephill Cove. Due to my pursuit of a fish and chip shop the night before, my walk this morning started off with a one and a half-mile trip along the A3055 to Freshwater Bay. I lightly cursed the need for such a detour from the coastal path, but after savouring the memory of the enormous meal I had scoffed and the lovely soft bed I had slept in, I reasoned that the extra three miles or so were well worth the effort, even if my toes did not agree with me.

Arriving back at Freshwater Bay, I left the short curved concrete promenade behind, to re-join the coastal path as it took me back up my first slope of the day, and past my first interesting observation of the morning. Just a few yards back on the grassland path I came across a small and rather touching memorial to a Second World War RAF pilot who had been lost just off the coast

of the Bay, in full view of the watching local population. A few
words described how one of ours had shot down one of theirs, but
then another of theirs had shot down ours in response. The
memorial looked fairly new, so I walked away thinking that maybe
some relations had finally found out where a long lost loved one
had perished all those years before. Cutting back onto the road as
the path edged round Freshwater cliff, I came across another
memorial. This time it was clearly quite recent as it only consisted
of a few dying flowers. Seemingly placed at the roadside to mark
the scene of another fatality on this fast stretch of the longest
section of almost straight road on the island. There was no name
with the flowers, but the sense of loss was just as tragic as the one
of over half a century before.

I crossed back onto the path again, and saw what was probably the most graphic illustration of the effect that coastal erosion was having on the entire island. Looking along the coastline to the southeast for as far as my eyes could see, I could make out great areas of browny-green murkiness in the sea, where the soft cliffs were being swept away by the alarmingly advancing sea. Back in 1983 I remember a large landslip at the other end of the beach at Blackgang Chine, but the preceding coastline was not too badly affected. In fact, there had then been quite a strong shingle beach that I crunched along instead of walking over the cliffs. Looking down now I could see there was far less knee-sapping shingle left, and that it had frequently been covered by sand from the eroded cliffs. Back in 1983, I also remember how the trip along this stretch of the island had been the longest and hottest part of the walk. It was my second day then as opposed to my third day now, I had picked up few blisters, and whenever possible I had broken into a steady jog wherever the conditions allowed. When it became too hot I just jumped into the sea to cool off for a few minutes, before marching off again for some more long hot miles.

Reaching the car park at Shippards Chine, I could see that not everyone had been deterred from taking a dip in the carrot-soup-sea below. A party of school kids was larking around fully clothed in the waves, oblivious to the muck they were jumping about in, or the ear-bashings that would no doubt follow when they got home. A few people were also eating ice creams while taking in the view from the car park, but looking at the edge of the cliff close by I could see it would not be long before coastal erosion would consume the car park itself. The barbed wire fencing was already hanging in mid-air in some places. It was easy to predict that another place would soon have to be found for ice cream vans and cars to park and admire the beautiful panoramic views from the Needles to St Catherine's lighthouse.

The path continued on its way along the cliffs, taking me past an old woman knitting, then past a proud seabird perched on top of a large rock just off the coast at Hanover Point. The large rock also marked the point where some of the best fossil finds on the island could be made. This fact was reinforced with every further inch of erosion, as the layers of crumbling cliffs revealed new finds for the small army of dinosaur hunters milling up and down in the area marked on the map as the 'Fossil Forest'. I felt the urge to drop down onto the beach and see what I could find too. However, I figured that the height of the holiday season was probably not the best time to go tramping up and down with my back bent double and my eyes fixed to the sand like all the others there that day. Instead, I just made a mental note to try and visit Brook Bay again at a better time of the year, in the early spring, after a few storms have hastened the erosion process.

Maybe I should have dropped down onto the beach at that stage, for I quickly regretted not doing so as the previously smooth path became very broken and pockmarked again after the absence of any significant rainfall. I could also see that the cracks and troughs were not helping to keep the cliffs in one piece. The lack of moisture was in effect working in tandem with the waves, shattering the ground with heat and dryness before the sea sucked it all out into the channel to start making more layers of sandstone and new fossils. This part of the coastline must have been one of the most isolated sections on the island. I did not come across a single person walking in either direction for the next two or three miles. Even when I had to switch back to the road again to bypass Chilton Chine and the Isle of Wight Pearl Centre I saw no one else. Both places appeared deserted. I was tempted to go and try to rouse someone to sell me a bar of chocolate in the Pearl Centre, but I knew there was probably another place to stop for a snack a mile or so further on so I let everyone enjoy their lunchbreak in peace. I had never visited the Pearl Centre, and wondered where they obtained the pearls from, and what they produced with them. I made another mental note to visit the centre someday – by car!

A mile further on I came to Brighstone holiday centre, a typical Hi-De-Hi type affair, that had once boasted acres of rolling green fields between it and the clear dark sea – but which was now perched on the very edge of the muddy waters below. The path took me right to one of the flimsy-looking chalets, although I could not follow the path around it as the route had suggested, for that section was now languishing some seventy feet below on the beach! Swerving into the camp itself I bumped into a stout looking man of about fifty pushing a wheelbarrow full of building materials. We stood talking for a few minutes as he explained how much he was wasting his time fighting a continual battle to maintain chalets that were being constantly destroyed by coastal erosion. He pointed out to the sea and told me how he had played a game of football 18 years ago on a grass pitch that had now completely vanished – under an assault that was chewing away at the coastline in these parts at the rate of 16 or 17 feet per year! Walking away from the once prosperous holiday centre, I could not help but wonder how long the remaining yards would take to collapse in to the sea, and leave the man and his wheelbarrow with no more chalets to try and patch up for another holiday season.

Returning to the flat grassland path, I came across a man who looked about eighty years of age, who had stopped to drain the contents of a plastic bottle he held to his lips. The drink looked like blackcurrant squash – but, because of the roguish grin on his old weathered face, it could have easily been something much stronger. Thinking of beverages reminded me that it was nearly time to quench my own thirst with the half litre of Royal Standard water that I had brought along. Half a litre may not sound much, but on a three hour walk I figured it should be enough to see me through to lunchtime, and then hopefully I could have something a lot more refreshing than just plain water. Thinking of a lunchtime break also made me think of my feet. My left big toe was aching quite a bit, and so was my right heel, but I was more fearful of what else I might find if I pulled my trainers off. I just hoped my feet were not damaged as badly as they felt, and pressed on for about two miles to yet another campsite. Reaching the assortment of coloured tents, I saw a few campers lounging around outside sunbathing. I gazed enviously at them for a short while, and considered briefly why I was torturing myself in this manner when these sensible people were just un-zipping their tents each morning to step outside and get the same suntan that I was walking over seventy miles to accumulate.

Shortly after leaving the campsite, I came across a less familiar site on my tour – an abandoned sewage treatment plant, complete with a large round silo of filtering gravel and a rusting, spinning sprinkler system that looked like an old derelict fairground ride. The sewage had obviously been pumped elsewhere for a number of years, probably because of the coastal erosion, and also because better ways had been found of disposing of such waste – rather than just flushing it straight into the sea.

I studied the map for the umpteenth time, and was increasingly pleased to fold over the sections to reveal more and more coastline advancing from the east – and fewer and fewer miles to walk until my lunchtime break. Reaching Cowlease Chine and then Shepherd's Chine I was even so elated that I thought I could spare some time to re-dress my feet for the final leg of the journey. I found a nice quiet spot by a trickling stream, and gingerly peeled off my trainers, socks and zinc oxide tape to reveal further damaged toes – and also a blister on my right heel the size of half an olive. This particular blister had not burst like the previous ones, and the pressure building up was quite clearly the reason for the pain, which had really started to throb over the past two or three miles. I knew of only one way of curing this pain – by bursting the blister and letting the pressure out. "But burst it with what?" I thought. I did not have a needle or a knife with me, and the skin was too thick to break with my fingernails alone. Searching around the ground where I sat with my foot in the air, I soon found a potential answer – albeit a rather Stone Age one in the shape of a small sharp flint that I quickly rinsed off to make a very primitive scalpel. With a quick incision the blister had been lanced and the liquid pain ebbed away before my eyes. I spent a further ten minutes patching up my feet using all the zinc oxide tape that I had left. I was sure that one last slog should see me finish the trip, and then I could attend to the damage more hygienically.

Climbing out of the sheltered Chine, I was struck by how cold it had become during my foot-break. Not only had my body cooled down, but the sky had clouded over and the wind had picked up enough to start pushing me back in the direction I had just come from! It was so cold in fact that I quickly put my T-shirt back on as I entered a strip of tall bending wild oats growing at the edge of a large field. It was just as well that I did too, for amongst the deep, billowing wild crop I came across a pair of elderly ladies enjoying a picnic lunch on a large tartan travel rug.

"There's a very unpleasant bean field up ahead. Best of luck!" they called out merrily as I swept past wondering what unearthly hazards I could encounter in a field full of beans. What sort of beans were they – runner beans, baked beans or an Isle of Wight killer variety? I soon found out what the ladies had been warning me about, though it was not so much the type of beans that was the problem – just the sheer size of the field they were in. The 'broad beans' seemed to go on and on forever in an endless mass of tangled stems and shoots, dragging at my ankles with each step I took. Quite fond of broad beans, I even tried to eat a couple of pods. But these were not the luscious, sweet types I used to pinch from my old grandad's garden. These were skinny, dry, sour varieties that I quickly spat out in disgust, preferring to wait a little longer for a sweeter feast.

Up on the approaching hill in front of me I could now more clearly see the two most distinctive features on that part of the high coastline overlooking St Catherine's Point. The Salt and

Pepper pots of Niton Down, also known as Chale Mountain, are two structures that were erected in the distant past to warn mariners of the dangers on the rocks below. One is tall and thin like a salt pot, and the other is short and fat like a pepper pot. The sight of them made the prospect of my journey's end even more certain, as I had visited the sites during one of my long training walks in the days leading up to the actual circumnavigation attempt. From their lofty position, I knew I had only a couple of miles to go to Niton, and then a further three miles to the finishing line. With that cheery thought in my mind I quickened my pace again and sped off as fast as my half-mummified toes would carry me – through the end of the bean field at Whale Chine and along the final mile of path and road to a watering hole I had heard so much about, that was an oasis for walkers who have just come from Freshwater Bay – about 11 miles away. Only this was not for the midday lunchbreak I had originally envisaged, as the time was now just passing two o'clock, and it was almost time for afternoon tea!

The Wight Mouse at Chale has a wide reputation as a good family pub for tourists and locals alike. Stepping inside, with a windblown and sun-scorched face, it was easy to see why. The old coaching inn had the look and feel of a place that said, 'come in and have drink and make your self at home'. That is exactly what I did for the next half an hour, as I propped my stick and backpack up against the bar, pointed at the cider pump and said to the barmaid, "I'll have two of those please."

The girl replied that they had two different types of cider, so I ordered one of each, and drained the first one while she poured the second from a bottle. I also ordered two Snickers bars, and then sat back on a high stool to enjoy them and people-watch around the bar. The first pint of cider barely touched the sides of my throat, but the second tasted as though it had been made with Calvados apples from France. It was so nice in fact that I quickly rinsed the chocolate away with the last drops and ordered another pint.

I could tell how popular the Wight Mouse was, for even at almost half past two the place was still full of holidaymakers enjoying late lunches, cooing over babies and rubbing suntan cream into wriggling youngsters. Then there were the local fraternities too. Small groups of farmers and men with the stance of squires, with sunburnt faces and weathered hands, clutching pints of cider, beer or gin and tonics to wash down their own lunches of two or three hours before. I felt so comfortable in the Wight Mouse I could have just stopped my walk there and then. But I knew I was nearing the end of my walk, so I left the bar to tackle the last leg of the trip – back to Steephill Cove.

Isle of Wight

CHAPTER SEVEN

CHALE TO STEEPHILL COVE

On the third day, at a quarter to three, I left the cool refreshing comfort of the Wight Mouse for the hot glare, blustery conditions and last foot-crunching leg of my second walk round the island. As usual my feet felt tired and sore, but now with less than half a day's walk remaining, I could not really care less about any discomfort inside my useless trainers. In fact, on the back of three pints of cider, I think I could almost have dispensed with the wretched things altogether and completed the last few miles barefooted. Leaving such fanciful dreams behind me, I made my way past the small village church, out of Chale and back onto the coastal path once more. After a short passage across a small field, this first section involved a nice gentle climb up the footpath adjacent to the Blackgang road as it swept upwards and just below the steep sides of Gore Down.

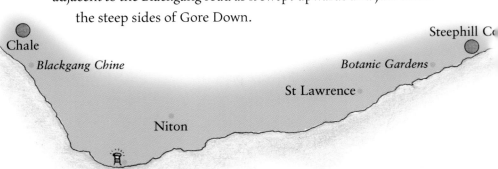

I passed the entrance to Blackgang Chine, with all its memories of so many family visits over the years, special visits normally paid in the hours of darkness, when the brilliant lights of the splendid old smuggling attraction are always at their most dazzling. A trip to Blackgang was an absolute must each year, and walking in the crisp early autumn night air was also a good way of cooling down after another long hot day making sandcastles on Ventnor beach. The only problem with Blackgang Chine is its location. This part of the coast may have been the best smuggling area on the island, but the crumbling cliffs are now slipping into the sea at an amazing rate.

Surprisingly, this dramatic erosion process has actually helped to keep Blackgang fresh and alive over the years. Instead of staying the same year in year out, the layout of the grounds has had to be constantly changed and moved further inland as the march of the sea has continued taking great chunks out of the land that Blackgang sits upon.

Continuing up the curling road, I eventually re-joined a cross-country path and arrived at a busy viewpoint, offering tremendous views back along the island's southwestern coastline to Dorset to my right, and St Catherine's Point below me to the left. To save a little weight, I had not brought a camera with me this time, whereas in 1983 I had taken a Kodak Instamatic. A little less than a mile after leaving the viewpoint, the distant views of Freshwater Bay and Tennyson Down gradually faded away as I followed the narrow cliff-edge path around Gore Cliff to West Cliff. Here all I could see were sights of the approaching coastline ahead of me up to St Boniface Down, above Ventnor. My route

I walked up and down with the water lapping around my knees for a good ten minutes or so, trying to summarise what I had achieved. I had started the adventure in search of fresh air, exercise and the solitude to recover from the emotions of the recent commemorative events that I had attended to mark the twenty-fifth anniversary of the Falklands War. Walking round the Isle of Wight for a second time, I think I had found all three. The walk had rubbed my toes to shreds, but the discomfort had not been in vain, for the sense of achievement outweighed any amount of blistered toes. I had not only completed everything that I had set out to achieve, I had also seen how much the Isle of Wight had to offer. Although it may never be the same old seaside hot spot as before, and coastal erosion is nibbling away at its edges, there are plenty of signs around that this lovely little island still has lots to offer future generations. Less than two hours from London, the Isle of Wight boasts just about the best sunshine record in the country. With no motorways or major traffic jams to worry about, it offers an amazing place of sanctuary for those stuck in the rat race on the other side of the Solent. So close to the heart of the country and for that matter Europe, it is within easy and affordable reach. Walking out of the sea and slowly back up the steps, I squelched my way back along Love Lane and into mum's garden, whereupon I kicked off the terrible trainers, took off the blood-stained socks, and tossed the whole wet bundle in the bin. That really was the best possible way to end my latest circum-navigation of the Isle of Wight. Throw away the old and look forward to the new – on one of the best little islands in the world.

The End